Miracles

Miracles

Do You Believe in Miracles?

*And God has placed in the church first of all
apostles, second prophets, third teachers, then
miracles, then gifts of healing, of helping, of
guidance, and of different kinds of tongues.*

1 Corinthians: 12:28 NIV

Miracles

From the author:

Some people believe that miracles happen, perhaps once in a lifetime, or sometimes on a daily basis; others believe that amazing events are only coincidences.

In this book, ordinary people open their hearts to recount miraculous episodes that have taken place in their lives. Some are life-changing, others are meeting a need, others are incredible answers to prayer.

If you do believe in miracles, this book will encourage you. If you do not believe, perhaps this book will change your mind.

In 'Do You Believe in Miracles', ordinary people tell their extraordinary stories.

Miracles

Introduction

My son's very existence is a miracle.

After an ectopic pregnancy put an end to our hopes of a family, and doctors and specialists told us there was no possibility of having a child naturally, it took twenty years for me to finally accept childlessness, to stop blaming God, and to accept God's plan for my life. Only then did God intervene and my son, Ryan was born.

But that's not the miracle I want to tell you about.

The miracle of Ryan's healing affected a lot of people. Many of those who had been praying for him thousands of miles away then emailed to say how blessed they had been by his healing and how it had encouraged them in their faith and in their own walk with God.

It has been four years since Ryan was healed, and I have had a recurrent thought since then. If one miracle can encourage so many in their faith, then perhaps there are other stories of life-changing miracles that need to be told.

Stories that can encourage believers, and perhaps open the hearts and minds of unbelievers.

So here they are.

Be blessed.

Healed By Faith

1

Ryan's Story.

When Ryan went off to university my husband and I decided the time was right to fulfil one of our own dreams and spend time in Spain.

My husband had been forced to take early retirement through ill health and our circumstances meant we could not afford to live in our house.

So we sold all our furniture, found tenants for the house, and moved into a caravan where we intended to live during the summer and spend the winters in Spain, the rental income providing us with sufficient money to live on, if we were frugal.

The first winter was anything but the dream we had anticipated. Firstly, my mother died suddenly, giving me no time to return home to be with her in her final hours.

Shortly after we had returned to Spain following her funeral I received a call from Ryan saying he had a large lump the size of a goose egg on his neck. He was feeling unwell, and the GP had arranged for him to see a Consultant at the local hospital in a newly opened clinic called the Neck Lump Clinic.

The appointment was in a few days so whilst Chris stayed in Spain to pray with our church family there, I returned home to accompany Ryan to the clinic.

It was a difficult time. Our home was rented out and the caravan site was closed for the winter. As Ryan was not feeling well I wanted him to stay with me rather than in his university digs, so we checked into a local guest house and waited for the hospital appointment.

It transpired that Ryan was the very first patient at the clinic, and the Consultant was very kind and considerate, but he was clearly perplexed by the lump which was solid and appeared to be getting bigger rapidly.

Ryan was sent for an immediate biopsy.

I am somewhat ashamed to say that I was a complete wreck, consumed with negative thoughts and fears, and somewhat bizarrely Ryan ended up holding my hand and comforting me as the needles and other paraphernalia were inserted in his neck.

He kept telling me that God was in control, and whilst I marvelled at his faith, I didn't believe it myself.

After the biopsy was taken we returned to the Consultant. He said the results would take about fourteen days, but he wanted to be honest and say that prior tests had ruled out the usual conditions such as Glandular Fever and other possible causes, and that we needed to be aware that the news may not be good.

I pushed for more clarification. Was he saying it was cancer? He refused to confirm this but his look told me that was what he was thinking.

He said that Ryan should let him know if the lump got any bigger and they would have him in straight away for surgery. His concern was clear.

To my surprise, Ryan asked if he could go and join his father in Spain as he felt the strain of waiting fourteen days would be eased if he could get away.

He probably thought that my state of mind would not help, either, although he was polite enough not to say that.

At first the Consultant was reluctant, but eventually it was decided that I would stay in England so that the hospital could contact me if the results of the biopsy came back early.

As Ryan departed for Spain I went back to the caravan site to see if I could get some of my clothes from the caravan, although I still had no idea where I would stay.

As I waited in the site manager's office all my fears and concerns came to a head and I broke down in tears. The manager was wonderful and ended up insisting I stay in one of their holiday caravans.

There were lots of walks on the caravan site and I spent many hours walking and praying, imploring God to intervene, even trying to bargain my life for my son's.

It was a cold and bleak winter and my faith was rock bottom.

In order to pass the time and to take my mind off our situation I decided to go through some of my mother's things, packing up items and mementoes I wanted to keep.

I came across her Bible and as I opened it I saw that on the first page she had written – Proverbs 3 v 3. I was surprised that she would have written a text reference, and it seemed very out of character.

When I turned to the text, I was amazed to read

"Take your love and faithfulness and bind it around your neck".

I doubt there are that many references in the Bible to 'neck'. This was no coincidence.

I immediately called Ryan and told him to read the text as I felt it was specifically for him. He then told me that he was going to our local church in Spain that night where they were going to anoint him with oil and pray for him.

Unbeknown to me, at the same time a prayer chain had been started for Ryan and people across the world were praying for his recovery, specifically that the lump on his neck would disappear.

I began to receive emails from people in Canada and America and Spain and England, all who were fervently praying for Ryan. I again felt ashamed at my lack of faith, and began to pray believing that my son would be healed.

A couple of days later Ryan called me to say that the lump was getting smaller. It was now the size of a hen's egg and was not as hard as it had been. He was finally able to hold his head straight, as until then his head had been on one side because the size of the lump prevented him from holding his head up. He also was feeling much better.

By the time he returned home for the hospital appointment, the lump had completely disappeared.

The Consultant at the hospital admitted he was baffled.

He told us that the test results had been inconclusive but on examining Ryan said that only good things go down. He was surprised, but pleased.

Ryan told him frankly that God had healed him. The Consultant paused briefly at that, but then said he could offer no other explanation, shook Ryan's hand, and discharged him.

So many people who had been praying for Ryan were blessed by his healing. I learned a valuable lesson, too. I had been so consumed with fear that

God couldn't get through to me, so I believe he used that verse in my mother's Bible to wake me up, open my heart, and restore my faith.

'The Lord has allowed me to live'

2

Michael's Story

Raised in Central Indiana farm country as an independent farm worker on about 200 acres, I had always been healthy and strong, in fact stronger than most classmates in all of my school days.

Ability developed to handle the unexpected challenges of farm operations, growing crops, raising several head of livestock, and all of the equipment operations needed to make it happen can be challenging to experienced adults let alone teen and preteen young boys.

As life sometimes proves, other events often interrupt our personal plans. Changes had altered my farm life and different occupations had been offered that unexpectedly changed my directions, yet I had been able to overcome and survive every challenge that I had ever been faced with until April 12, 1976.

On that day at age 33, married with three young daughters, I found myself unemployed, without any health insurance and suddenly experienced a severe pain that struck between my shoulder blades.

Thinking that I had somehow twisted my back out of temporary alignment I tried everything I could think of to ease the pain.

My wife was on an errand transporting a friend to her doctor appointment and our kids were in school so I was alone with pain severe enough to incapacitate me for over an hour.

I made it back to our living room to a chair to sit slumped over in the only position I could tolerate, barely able to breathe to wait for my wife's return.

On her arrival back home she discovered my ashen grey colour with profuse sweating condition and took me to our doctor's office who immediately directed us to the hospital.

Having never been admitted to a hospital, I was surprised how emergency room staff quickly wired and plumbed me for monitoring then gave me several nitro-glycerine pills which did nothing for the pain.

Next a nurse came with a syringe full of morphine which provided relief from the pain, but also with the fuzzy, surreal dreamy experience of an induced coma.

My next memorable experience was the next morning waking to a doctor near my face with a loud voice telling me, "*You were lucky - less than two young men out of a hundred your age even make it to a hospital, let alone live through the night with your condition!*"

I further discovered that my condition was called an "acute myocardial infarction", basically a very serious heart attack.

Then another cardiologist arrived with laboratory enzyme blood count results.

My enzyme blood counts were supposed to be between 135 and 170 but were 3,163 and should have resulted in my instant death.

The cardiologist told me *"The lab technician ran the test three times to be sure it was correct."*

He then also related to my wife and I that the monitoring system I was connected to also fed my heart data directly to the Krannert Institute of Cardiology in Indianapolis where my name was recorded as only the fifth man to live with that high a blood count.

The hospital stay and over seven months of recuperation time allowed enough healing for doctors to release me to take a job in sales without physical labour.

During this experience I became convinced that I needed to invite Jesus Christ into my life.

I was helpless, broke and hopeless yet when I spoke my invitation to God, what felt like a flood of internal warmth rose up me in every way. Peace replaced fear and a sense of calmness refreshed my soul.

I had looked into the Bible very few times in my life, but a near overwhelming desire to read and study the Bible came along with that change when Christ entered my life.

My early childhood church experience amounted to two.

One was the feeling that my parents dragged me to a Catholic wedding when I was preschool age, still in my memory as the longest most boring time of my life.

The second experience was just after entering first grade when a first-grade school buddy invited me to his church. Again, a bad impression when the preacher scolded me about my not knowing how to correctly shake his hand.

Those bad impression childhood memories had my defence built against anything and anyone church related and except for a few times attending much later because of a pretty teenage girl, I was able to avoid even knowing anything about God or what real faith was.

That teenage girl later became my wife and without realizing it also became instrumental in my accepting Christ in ICU (intensive care unit) in April 1976.

That peace like a river became very real and now after the last forty-one years has sustained me through my life.

About a year later a smaller repeat of the back pain symptoms returned and caused the cardiologists to order a 'heart catheterization' procedure where a long tube was fed through a surgical cut in my groin artery up into all parts of my heart.

Camera equipment provided the video of some special dye that was injected showing what had actually happened inside my heart to begin with.

No blockages were found but in the lower (inferior) section of my heart a weak spot about an inch long had ruptured toward my back.

It had healed over shown by the scar tissue that the doctor said was *"probably stronger than before, but evidence would always be seen on all future medical tests such as EKG's."*

Just a few years ago I was in the hospital for another short term condition and a cardiologist came into my room, introduced himself to my wife, oldest daughter and me with, *"Hello, I just wanted to drop in and chat with you a moment. I have been a cardiologist for over 25 years and looked at your history in the hospital records. I am amazed because I have never even heard of a man living with your condition very long. I have heard of a few women living for about 10 years but never a man and you're alive after more than 35 years, I think you are a miracle and wanted to personally meet you."*

He shook each of our hands.

I am not on any heart medications and have followed the doctor's recommendations to avoid over-exerting and getting extremely tired, watch my diet, and eat healthy.

Other than that; *"you'll know what you can't do and don't push it"* were my last instructions.

I do tire more easily and don't have the strength or endurance I remember having before, but other than that I survive as well as most others and still with that peace I never had before the attack.

During another experience almost ten years after the heart attack, while doing some maintenance work in a high school building, I was involved in a remodelling project of a science classroom involving mechanical utilities.

I was removing some and moving some 'supposedly disconnected' electrical wiring.

The wiring was not shown on any documents and had been tested as 'dead' for electrical current, so my assumption was to simply cut the dead wires with my lineman electrician pliers to remove them.

Standing high up on a ten foot step ladder on the trashed floor of that remodel project I decided to take a hold of something substantial for more stability, so I grabbed hold of a steel bar joist above the ceiling and proceeded to cut the wires.

The wires were a part of a complicated four way switching system and when certain switches were in even what looked to be the off position, a part of the wiring system had what is called 'back feed'.

When I squeezed my cutters a surge of live 277 volts and 20 amperes went into my hand squeezing the pliers through my upper body to my other hand holding on the perfectly grounded steel bar joist.

I screamed the name of Jesus as I passed out.

When I came to I was sitting on the cement floor in water, propane gas and drain pipes each about a foot above the cement for the science desks.

Miracles

I was shaking all over with a taste like burnt toast in my mouth and noise in my ears like an out of tune radio on a stormy night.

Only God knows how my unconscious body could fall into the dangerous floor area without serious injury.

The school principal called the doctor's office for me and the doctor said; *"Well, you are talking to me so I don't think I can help you with anything because you survived alive. Go get some rest."*

I still have scar tissue near my right thumb from burns of the pliers and voltage shock.

The smaller pepper looking burns on my left hand holding onto the steel bar joist have healed completely but the memory of voltage going through me is unforgettable.

I have no reason or justification as to why I have been spared except that the Lord has for His own reasons blessed me and allowed me to live.

Now on my way to age 75 and still with the peace that passes understanding I still have the hunger to understand and study scripture.

Our family has grown. Our three daughters now have eight grandchildren with ten great grandchildren and so many friends have blessed my life.

I believe that our God is the only one to know the answer as to "why". It is just that to me He does. "I do believe in miracles and believe that I am one of the Lord's."

+

Mike Selch is a lifelong native of central Indiana agriculture country, married 55 years with three daughters, eight grandchildren and nine great grandchildren (at this point). Always been a "hands on" type guy and enjoyed the challenges to fix or improve whatever problems encountered, or discover reasons why.

In providing for family several fields and trades have included farming, insurance, racing, truck driver, construction, education, municipal government, ordained minister and now author. Retirement is providing opportunity to share a few of the experiences of overcoming some of the life challenges including health problems, with hopes of helping and encouraging others.

Mike is the author of Finding Peace About Death, which he describes as - How I found peace about death of loved ones, family and friends and when facing death myself. Hoping to help others find peace when distressed by a death.

Michael Selch. Indiana

Prophecy Fulfilled

3

Eileen's Story – Prophesy Fulfilled.

A disturbing occurrence had happened to our family unit and I as a mother was very sad at the time.

This particular weekend, my husband and I were staying with our son and daughter-in-law at their house in Chepstow, and we were all together in the church they attended on Sunday mornings, namely Kings Church, Newport, Gwent, in Wales.

Being sad and upset by recent events, I responded, along with many others, to the offer given by Ray

Bevan, the Pastor, to go down the front of the church for prayer.

After joining the prayer queues and receiving prayer, and with mascara running down my cheeks due to crying a lot,

I turned around to go back to my seat to re-join my family when I saw a face on the front row of seats that I knew so well, that of Tony Gardener, a giant of a man, a farmer from Shelfanger, near Diss in Norfolk.

He was a man previously known for having a terrible temper, but who was totally changed when he gave his heart and life to Jesus.

We were now living in Wales, but when we were living in Norfolk Tony was a good friend of ours and our two families fellowshipped together in Mount Zion Church in Norwich.

Tony was a strong supporter of the Norwich Chapter as well as the Diss Chapter of the Full Gospel Businessmen's Fellowship International Organisation, travelling to Africa and other countries to tell people how Jesus changes lives, and God used him greatly to perform miracles.

Composing my tearful self, I said, "Hello Tony, what are you doing here?" thinking the counties of Norfolk and Gwent are on opposite sides of Great Britain.

Tony responded. "I was the speaker at the FGBMFI meeting here yesterday."

I said to Tony "David (my husband), Martin and Eirian (my son and daughter-in-law) are up there," pointing to the higher level of the building, where they were seated, and Tony said "Call them down," which I did by motioning with my hands for them to come down to the front of the church.

As soon as everybody had hugged each other, and without any conversation, Tony said "Let's all hold hands," which we did in a circle, and in closing our eyes out came these words from Tony's mouth, "My daughter, I have heard your prayer and I can see a pink bonnet."

Well I was stunned, you can imagine my surprise.

I thought he was going to pray for me, as I had been the one crying down the front of the church, asking for prayer, but no, he was delivering a message direct from God to our daughter-in-law, Eirian.

Eirian you see had previously lost five pregnancies in different stages of gestation and being so discouraged she had previously said to our son, Martin that they should try once more and then forget it.

Some weeks before that, when they were visiting us for the weekend, Martin told me what Eirian had said to him and the words that came out of my mouth were perhaps a little brusque as I heard myself saying "Tell Eirian not to play God."

Not long after Tony prophesising the birth of a baby girl to Eirian, we learnt that our daughter in law was pregnant and a date in April was advised as the expected arrival.

So each day I covered her in prayer as I drove to and from work, a journey of circa fifteen minutes. I knew how many months, then how many weeks and then how many days there were left before the guesstimated date of birth.

At the full nine months, when again we happened to be at Martin and Eirian's house for the weekend, Eirian said on the Saturday afternoon, "I think the baby is coming shortly," having had no previous experience to be confident to make that statement.

Eirian was right though, as unbeknown to me as I was wearing earplugs in bed and my husband who slept like a log, Eirian went into labour that night, and Martin had called the midwife. We were totally oblivious of all that was going on, and we woke to find them just leaving the house to go to hospital in Newport.

My husband and I got washed and dressed and went to Kings Church in Newport in the morning and hung around the town during the day, popping into the hospital every so often to get updates.

We went to the evening church service as well, calling afterwards at the hospital and settled down in the corridor waiting for further news.

So we were there when Martin came out of the delivery ward and excitedly said "the baby has arrived."

Eirian had given birth to a wonderful, healthy baby girl, whom they later named Nia.

The first person my husband and I phoned when we got back to our house to tell of Nia's birth was Tony Gardener, so he should know that the prophesy that God gave him to deliver had been wonderfully fulfilled.

His wife Jean answered the phone, as Tony was not at home at the time, and we said please tell Tony that Eirian has had a beautiful baby girl, as per the prophesy given by Tony.

Jean, his wife said, "You know Tony knew nothing about Eirian and Martin's desire to become parents."

I said "We know..there was absolutely no communication between any of us, that morning or any time previously", but of course Eirian had prayed to God and He had heard her prayer and He gave her an audible message via Tony Gardener to tell her so.

So, dear reader, God spoke and it was so and Nia is now a beautiful young lady, she is beautiful inside and beautiful outside.

In her late teens, after always accompanying her parents to church, she made her own decision and became a born-again Christian.

Nia took a year out before commencing university, working five months in Malawi in Africa with Tearfund, as a volunteer, before commencing Bath university to study pharmacy.

Before going to Malawi she said God had specifically told her to go to a non-european country and the two filtered options offered to her by Tearfund were South Africa and Malawi. Nia said, "I will go where God sends me," and He sent her to Malawi.

She said that living, working and teaching the Malawian ladies with health advice, agricultural techniques , physically working in the fields with them, sharing Jesus with them, and being invited to eat with them was a very humbling but very rewarding experience.

Nia´s birth was specifically prophesised by God. He never said to her mother, Eirian, "You will have a baby."

He was specific. He said it would be a girl by using the words "I can see a pink bonnet" so there was no risk of chance on the gender of the baby.

A girl He said and a girl He gave.

Dear reader, the Creator of the universe still hears and cares for individuals and is still performing miracles today.

God is the same yesterday, today and forever.

Never doubt it.

+

Born and educated in Middlesex, in the United Kingdom, I married at a young age my childhood sweetheart, David. We actually attended the same infant and junior schools, commencing school just before five years of age.

We have had two children, first a son then eleven years later, a daughter. Now God has blessed us with five grandchildren.

We have lived in England then the South of France, where my husband built us a house on the Mas de Bouis mountain in St Martin de Londres, Herault. We have lived in two different areas of Wales and have lived in southern Spain since 1998, where we attend an English-speaking Pentecostal church on Sunday mornings and a very lively Spanish church, with gypsy music in the evenings.

I became a born again Christian at the age of 21 years after being encouraged by my sister, Annette, to go along and listen to the American evangelist, Billy Graham, whose campaigns were broadcast live from London to a huge screen set up in Norwich in Norfolk. My sister had gone along to see and hear him live in London and said "You must go and listen to what he has to say."

I went for the three nights that there were broadcasts to Norwich and God moved me so much each night I could not easily tell my husband what I had heard, but on the third and final night I made my decision.

A veritable, palpable battle had gone on in my legs, one force trying to hold me down in my seat and another force pushing me up, but God won the battle in the force pushing me up and I found myself walking down to the front, at the huge cinema-like screen . I said the sinner's prayer along with other people who had responded to Billy Graham's altar call, following the words that he said, phrase by phrase and Halleluiah I had been born again by the spirit of God, and I knew it.

I cried for around forty-five minutes. Tears of joy; tears of repentance; tears of cleansing; only God knows why but the next day the sun seemed brighter and the flowers more colourful.

I had peace with God and He was my father, my Lord, my saviour and I have learned through these fifty odd years that have passed since then, that He is my best friend.

Nobody but Billy Graham had explained so clearly to me why Jesus had left heaven to come to earth to suffer at the hands of humans...it was to save my soul, to reconcile me to God and to have a personal relationship with me, and He would have done it even if it was just for me, to die on a cross where my sins would be covered and forgiven.

That was over 51 years ago..praise God..I have seen God do miracles in so many ways in our family, and in our businesses, we know He hears and He acts. He is our loving father and He cares.

If you know that you do not have a personal relationship with God, I would encourage you to give Him your life, it will never be unfulfilled and there will be a place prepared for you in heaven, where God tells us in the Bible that we shall have no aches or pains, no suffering, eternal bodies and where we can enjoy the presence of God eternally.

What a marvellous prospect, friend. It is certain that we were not here on earth 100 years ago and we won't be here in 100 years, so don't take this life too seriously. We are only passing through.

Remember it does not matter where we have come from, but it certainly matters where we are going. There is a heaven to gain and a hell to spurn the Bible tells us.

The decision is yours though. Remember that God´s arms are open wide but you need to be the one running to Him, just like the prodigal son did.

Eileen Alma Templeman

Testimony of Healing

4

Julie's Story – Testimony of healing

They were the words we all dread to hear. "I´m afraid you have cancer in the breast, it is aggressive and serious, and has travelled to the lymph nodes".

Surely not me, I am still young, it can´t be, words jumbling around in my head. I´m afraid that at the beginning I went to pieces because I knew from the way the doctor had relayed the news to me that it was very serious.

But then, my sister who lived in Marbella, Spain, knowing that the Spanish mail system was "donkey pace" slow, travelled to Gibraltar to send me a little book called "Healed of Cancer" by Jodie Osteen. I have ordered dozens of this book since to give out to people diagnosed with cancer. It was to be a very powerful influence in my life because it tells how Dodie fought and won her battle with liver cancer by standing on the Word of God.

I am not of the "name it and claim it" brigade, but as I read this book, the Word of God started to resonate inside me and faith started to grow.

It helped that I received a definite Rhema Word from the Lord from John 10 : 10. *The devil comes only to rob, kill, steal and destroy, but I have come so that you may have life in all its fullness.*

So I knew this was a demonic attack, and that I had not lived my appointed days according to Psalm 139. And so, knowing that and armed with my Rhema Word, I started to fight the devil the only way I knew how, by using my sword, the Word of God.

I found as many scriptures on healing that I could (Dodie´s book helped enormously in this), I wrote them on small cards and I put them everywhere that my eyes would fall. By my bed, by the kettle, by the sink, where I sat in the evenings, in the bathroom, literally everywhere I could think of and

I would meditate on them speak them out, walk them, talk them, until I was immersed in them, and as I did faith grew in me.

It was so good to have something positive to concentrate my mind on because from the physical aspect, nothing was working. I lost weight, I was very ill, I had surgery, chemotherapy, massive doses of radiotherapy, and finally, morphine, injected, liquid (Oramorph) and slow release tablets (M.S.T)

 I was in and out of Hospital as my body began to break down and I knew I was dying.

Until, finally, back into hospital which we all knew was for the last time.

A couple of mornings later, a Tuesday, a doctor came to tell me that the next morning I was to be transferred to the Hospice as there was nothing more they could do for me.

All that they had been doing was giving me strong morphine injections. I was so upset and quite desperate and having a lot to do to get my affairs in order, I asked them how long I had. The answer - two weeks at the outside.

I was completely devastated, I had had such faith for my healing, had stood my ground against the devil, had wielded my sword, the Word of God, against him tirelessly. I was desperate, in fact very angry with God. I shouted at Him "I have prayed for so many people who have been healed, where are You when I need you?"

Then it happened. I was filled with cool air, which somehow, I knew came from a long way off, it came through my head and gradually worked its way down through my body to my feet, and I thought I had actually died. After all I didn't know what death felt like, perhaps it is like being filled with cool air.

But I didn't see Jesus (*John 14 : 3*)   and if I was dead, how could I still see the other patients in the Ward, I couldn't work it out, and so I slept.

When I woke the next morning, something had radically changed. My body was still emaciated, they were still injecting me with morphine, but I KNEW IN MY SPIRIT THAT I WAS NO LONGER DYING!!

I asked the Doctor if I could wait a few days before going to the Hospice and she said I could. Well, I never went into the Hospice and I came out of hospital two weeks later, supposedly in remission which the Doctors couldn't understand, but I knew I was healed, that God in His power and mercy had done it!

Upon returning home I shared with my Spiritual Warfare Group (another amazing story in itself and one about which I am at present writing a book) the story of what had happened that Tuesday in the hospital.

They were amazed and said, "Julie, the Holy Spirit told us to come together and pray for you that very day, go and look in the diary and see how He led us to pray".

In this group, we prayed only what we believed the Holy Spirit gave us and we kept a diary. That Tuesday the Holy Spirit told them to pray this, "Father will you fill Julie's body with Your breath, the Breath of Life"! That cool air that passed through me was nothing less than the Breath of God Himself, Hallelujah! I was healed of Breast and Lymphatic cancer.

The story doesn't end there. When I came out of Hospital I was completely addicted to morphine, and I couldn't function without it. For nine months, I tried to stop it and each time would just land back in Hospital, and back on morphine.

Until one day my Church were going by coach to a meeting at Wembley, Bennie Hinn was the Speaker. I was too ill to go on the coach (the morphine was literally killing me) so my husband took me in the car. He had to carry me to the car and carry me into the auditorium. During the singing of an old Hymn, a 15-year-old boy put his hand on my shoulder and I felt the electricity of the Holy Spirit going through my body, it was an amazing experience. But I didn't really know exactly what was going on. I was duly brought home and for the first time in months, slept without morphine.

The next morning I said to my husband "I don't feel too bad this morning so I won't take the morphine until I need it". I HAVE NOT HAD A GRAMME OF MORPHINE FROM THAT DAY TO THIS. I was completely delivered from Morphine addiction! Praise God! - and I do daily.

When I was facing death, and despite trusting God, I experienced the worst terror imaginable. All I could see ahead of me was a great black hole and I remember saying to my husband, "Soon you will be here, the Church will be here, the Clinic will be here, the family will be here, but where will I be?" I imagined falling into this black hole not knowing what horrors lay there.

After I was healed, I asked the Lord why I went through that terror, and His reply was: "Because I wanted you to experience what it is like for unbelievers when they face death, because having experienced it, you will never stop telling people about Me." And I never have.

To complete the story, I have had another dose of cancer since, had a lot of surgery and treatment, but not in the breast and not in the lymph system, and I am still alive and well to tell the tale!! What a mighty God we serve.

Julie, formerly a professional singer, married her husband Robin in 1979, and they had a music ministry together in the 1980's. They were called to Spain in 2010 where Robin is Pastor of New Life Church. Their church website is newlifechurch.eu

Juliet Hawkins

God is my Provider

5

Jan's Story -God is my provider

Just over five years ago I moved from the Isle of Wight, a place I had lived all my life, to work for a church in Norfolk.

God clearly showed me He was leading me. He sold my home without me advertising it for sale, and found me a flat here with all the things from my "wants list", i.e. secure entry, 2 bedrooms, a bath in the bathroom and a small outside space.

The role of children and family worker was as near perfect as I'd ever dreamed. I used to go home and pinch myself to see if it was real, I loved it so much.

Sadly, just over a year later I resigned, as a new church leader brought change and we found it impossible to work together so I was left with little option but to resign.

That was a very low time in my life – giving up my job, which meant no income and no income meant no flat (that I had also loved!)

Reverend Andrew and his wife, Carol, kindly offered me a room in their fab home, rent free. I could not have been made more welcome.

Whilst with them I tried to claim job seekers as I was now unemployed, but I was in such a bad way that I cried throughout my initial interview at the Job Centre that the advisor gently said: "I think you should see your GP and claim ESA!"

This I did for the next two months, and then thought I could milk this and stay on it a while. Uh! No!

I changed my claim to job seekers with every intention of getting a job.

TLC had started taking of my time when I had the energy to work on it. (TLC was a social enterprise my friend and I had started to reach the people in the community who would never step inside of church. TLC stands for Tender Loving Care).

Each fortnight I'd go to the job centre with a list of jobs I'd applied for and each fortnight I was given a different reason why I'd had no money.

I had differing opinions from my friends.

Some said "Benefits are God's provision you should have them," whilst others said I was a snob who doesn't want to sign on as unemployed, and still others like my dear friend Shelley, who said "Go with what you feel God is saying to you!"

And I felt strongly that God was saying, trust me.

So I rang the benefits office and cancelled my claim.

The lady at the end of the telephone asked "Is that some kind of training scheme?"

I replied "Yes, probably but not one you'd understand!"

I'd done it. I had taken a massive leap of faith. I had wrestled with the £5,000 that the church had offered me when the relationship between the new vicar and

I broke down but I just could not keep my integrity and sign a document to accept the monies.

So, I'd left without a penny, and now no benefits.

One day about seven months later, Andrew and Carol informed me they were moving out of area. I thought – God I hope you are in this. I opened my Bible and read: "My father's house has many rooms!" I knew God had my next home in hand.

A few hours later Reverend Linda came to pick me up. When I got in the car she said, "God has told me to offer you two rooms in my home", again rent free. Tears flowed. I just couldn't believe it. God is amazing I know, but He never ceases to amaze me!

I stayed with Linda for about a year, having one room as my bedroom and one room as an office base for TLC. Linda took on the baton of encouragement from Andrew and Carol encouraging me on the often painful and difficult journey of building the outreach project that had started to grow.

At that time I was volunteering full time, completely dependent on others for finance until the day came when the project was able to pay me a minimal income.

When it was time to move from Linda's I spent a hard month praying as another base did not open immediately. So, it was a case of "Where am I staying tonight Lord?" But, God provided a night here, a few days there. I was never left without a bed each night. But, it was tough and lonely.

One night as I was driving back to my bed for that particular night I cried out to God: "If you don't write it in the sky in lights you want me to stay I am going back to the Isle of Wight tomorrow!"

As I came to a roundabout I looked over to the Little Chef Café and saw that some of the lights were broken. The only lights showing were T L C (the name of the project I was building and leading).

I ignored it for two nights, on the third night I went back to get my friend Tracy to photograph it with me! I knew without doubt God was asking me to stay.

The following weekend our evangelism team took to the streets to share their faith with those they meet. As was usual my flesh was reluctant, but I knew once I was out I would be okay.

Mid-afternoon I received a call from one of the team, telling me he had met a friend who needed a cat and house sitter for two weeks and would I be interested? I didn't have to think about that!!! How I was praising God – two whole weeks in a house to myself for the cost of caring for 2 cats.

I met Rich (who was going on a ministry trip to South Africa), and his wife Marion (who was sadly nursing her dying mum in another area). Marion was really excited about TLC and hoped one day to join us. They told me they had been praying about having a lodger.

So, after the two weeks I asked if they would consider me as a lodger and praise God they agreed. They asked for only a small rent as they wanted to support my ministry.

It's never easy living with others and I have been on both sides of being a guest and having guests stay in my home.

I had come to realise that there comes a day when it just doesn't work – nobody needs to have done anything different or upset anyone it is just that God's grace lifts and it is time to part.

I was having breakfast one day with some friends when they told me they had been praying about me and would like to offer me a home with them, just at the point it was time to leave Rich and Marion's. However after a few months it was clear it wasn't working for either of us. So, I moved back to Rich and Marion's who welcomed me with open arms.

Then this amazing thing happened. Some friends offered to buy a house in Great Yarmouth town centre for me to live in "rent free" initially for one year.

What a blessing! A home of my own with a kitchen big enough for a small table, dining room, lounge and four bedrooms. Perfect!!

There was a little damp, making one bedroom totally unusable, and nights where I would wake petrified, which didn't seem to go despite my prayers, the prayers of others and anointing the room with oil.

But, the house gave me the opportunity to have friends to meals, start a Sunday evening fellowship and weekend sleepovers with Tracy and Dave. Plus I had a huge storage cupboard for the much needed resources for the homeless we had begun to work with.

At the end of the year, I began to feel more and more uncomfortable in the house and in my life. I cried out one morning to God to please bring some change! A few days later I received a text from the landlord giving me notice to leave. The property had been more costly than they had anticipated and they needed to rent it out to recoup some income.

Back to the prayer room. I was still only paid one day a week from the project that was now more than a full-time role for me.

Not sure what to do next I clung to: "God is my provider."

I applied for jobs but never received a response. My friend, Sue, had offered me a room in her home if nothing else materialised, so I texted her asking if she was serious.

She too said that she would not take any payment from me, and refused to cash a cheque when the council tax amounted to hundreds of pounds for having me in her home.

Now, as I write this I am once again wondering what is next. Funding is slowly coming in to increase my wage which is increasing next month to two days a week for two months.

Sue had kindly offered me three months, had extended it to six but I felt it was time to leave when six months turned to seven and a half.

We had booked four different homeless people into different B&B's over a weekend and I just felt in my spirit I needed to step out in faith.

My friend Dave approached a local Bed and Breakfast he uses in Great Yarmouth when he visits and they kindly offered me a deal for six weeks.

When Serene and Stanley, the owners, showed me round they offered me the best room at a reasonable rate and a smaller one for a lot less. As they are Christians they told me to go and pray about it.

With little income I wasn't sure what to do, until I read my daily reading entitled: "Lack Nothing" and it spoke of Jesus sending his disciples on their first ministry trip with nothing, and then another time told them to take their purse bag and cloak. And it ended questioning: Do we trust God to supply our needs?

I knew God would want me to have the best. So, I phoned Serene and booked the larger room, and felt a total peace come upon me.

A few days later when I left Sue's, storing my excess things at another friend's house, I was told by Serene that they would not be charging me for my first week at the B&B as they were giving it to me as a gift in support of the work of TLC Great Yarmouth!

It has been four amazing, tough years but as I look back God has provided every step of the way just as he promises in His Word.

+

I am the co-founder and manager of TLC GY which is a Christian outreach project in Great Yarmouth which has been running for nearly five years, and has recently been granted charitable status.

Our mission statement is: *'Bringing hope to the heart of the community!'* We do this through street teams, community groups and supporting individuals.

We also own a Double Decker bus which is being transformed into a flexible venue with kitchenette downstairs and meeting space upstairs.

We reach out to some of the most vulnerable members of the community – those struggling with or recovering from substance misuse, prostitutes, homeless, victims of domestic violence, lonely and the elderly.

The majority of our outreach is undertaken by volunteers. I am currently paid one day a week, and live by faith for the rest of my needs.

I love my role because I love people and enjoy sharing my faith with those I meet. It has been great to see lives changed with those who come to know Jesus and start to live a life with meaning and purpose.

Jan Tapp BA, Dip(HSW)

My wife said 'I am still alive.'

6

Jerry's Story

My wife, Marilyn, and I are retired missionaries from Spain.

We moved to Spain in 1999 because Marilyn was given one year to live by her doctors, because she had one of five diseases known in the world, back in 1999.

The two front lobs in her brain were turning to liquid and her brain was just dissolving and disappearing.

At that time 17% of her brain was missing and UCLA medical centre was trying to help with the many problems she was having living daily life and passing out during her high school teaching classes. All the while UCLA Medical staff was trying to find a way to stop this problem.

Our lives stopped, and it was an easy decision to make for her last year alive, to stop our lives and sell everything to move to a new country for Marilyn to live out her last days in a country she wanted to retire to someday.

Once in Spain, we found a strong need to be with Jesus and fellowship with likeminded Christians.

There were no Christian churches anywhere throughout the three towns surrounding our area of Spain, or in the little city we lived in, Mojacar.

We started a men's fellowship and then a women's fellowship and did not tell anyone about Marilyn's condition so people would come to be with Jesus.

In time our home and patio got too small for the home fellowships as well as it eventually turned into a Sunday service.

Eventually, we outgrew our patio and we started renting a larger place for the Sunday services to meet in.

As the years passed, we got the Spanish paperwork to be legal in Spain, for our first church in Mojacar.

Then we helped start many home fellowships and with our Lord's help we helped some to develop into their own church, two in the mountains of Albox and one in the city of Huercal Overa, all over one hour from Mojacar.

Along the way I joined the Crossroads Christian Bible College and Theological Seminary in 2001-2 and received my Pastoral Certificate..

Years later Marilyn had a dream that it was time for us to step down as founders and senior pastors, and we called for a blind fast from all four churches while not telling them why we were calling for a twenty-four hour fast and prayers.

We were wanting on our Lord to make that decision if this vision was from Him. as well as for Jesus to bring in the right pastors without us leading people in what to pray for and fast for.

Two weeks later a Northern Ireland pastor called to ask if he could help us in any way giving Sunday messages or even taking over the church as the pastor, if there was a need.

Our Lord answered our blind fast and prayers with a wonderful Pastor.

He stepped in as lead pastor and one year later he fully took over the Mojacar church and three other elders and pastors took over the other churches so they all would be self-sufficient on their own.

After a year, we returned to the United States.

During the flight, Marilyn leaned over to me and said: "I am still alive. We forgot completely about my death warrant!"

We had been so busy with our work for the Lord we had forgotten all about her brain condition.

Those years just seemed to fly by with no time left each day. Thank you, Jesus, what a wonderful gift for Marilyn.

And thank you to Jesus for allowing Marilyn and I to tag along with Him as He healed many and guided us to pray with many people who gave their lives over to Him.

Thank you to the Lord, for allowing us to be at His side to help assist Him all along that road and I want to thank Him for my blind faith in Him.

What a wonderful gift of life He gave Marilyn and what a wonderful gift of many years, and future years of shared moments with my wife, and especially with my Lord and Saviour.

We returned home and she went back to UCLA for a testing and she has 23% of her brain missing today, with some kind of liquid in its place.

The doctors looked at Marilyn and said you should not be here or living. Marilyn said to the doctor, "It is only by the grace of God that I am standing here, Jesus is real and I am His testimony to His miracle He gave me."

Our Lord had a different need for Marilyn and myself in this area as there were no evangelic style of churches here in our area of life, other than a Catholic church.

Today, we are busy giving messages in different churches on a regular basis in the Andalusia area of Spain.

When we are home in California, we start visiting with family in New York, Los Angeles, and San Diego. We join in several home fellowships within the area we live in while in the US. And time still keeps on passing us by so quickly!

Our Lord is just so wonderful, His future for us is wonderful, and it is up to us to follow without knowing what is next in our lives sometimes. Our Faith is our strength in loving Jesus.

I feel we are to be ready to help Jesus at any age and all the way up to that moment in time our Lord takes each one of us, home.

There will be just one more person to share Jesus's love with.

I always carry anointing oil in a small tube on my key ring, so we can pray for and anoint anyone, anywhere, at any time.

I ask Jesus to bring people to us any where we live,
and He does.

+

Bishop Dr Jerry Lee Garza Taylor, is Missionary
and Overseas Director of Colleges with Crossroads
Christian Bible College.

He lives with his wife, Marilyn, in Andalucia,
Spain.

Answers to Three Real Needs

7

David's Story – Answers to Three Real Needs

When I was doing some building work near Diss, in Norfolk, UK, being a self-employed builder, I needed to move my cement mixer from the job I had just finished to take it back to my yard.

As usual I put two wooden planks from the road onto my trailer and tried pulling the mixer up onto it with all my strength, but this time I did not have another worker to help me, and despite pulling with all my might, it never moved. I took a moment to rest and compose myself and tried again, the same effect, it never moved. I repeated the same procedure till I was quite exhausted and rather frustrated.

Then in the distance I could hear a heartening noise and upon looking up I could see it was a tractor coming in my direction. I said to myself, "Thank you, Lord," thinking that the driver could give me a hand, but to my enormous disappointment the tractor never came fully my way, but turned off down a lane well before where I was and the solution to my situation disappeared out of sight.

Being in the middle of the countryside and with nobody in sight or anybody in the owner's house at the time where I was working, I then prayed to God in desperation, "Please Lord help me get this cement mixer up onto my trailer, there is nobody around to help me."

It was only a short prayer, but it was a cry from the heart and despite being extremely tired from the numerous previous efforts, again standing on the trailer I pulled the cement mixer and to my utter amazement it 'flew' up the two wooden planks and was on my trailer in the blink of an eye.

I just stood there absolutely stunned and thanked God so much because of the reality that He should answer my need so rapidly and so miraculously.

When I have told people of this event I have asked myself if I had unseen angels helping me. I have to say I think so, there was no other explanation. I was in the middle of nowhere, exhausted and totally devoid of any human assistance.

On another occasion, I had a real need again that God answered. For many weeks I had been with another self-employed bricklayer building a bungalow near Diss in Norfolk and I needed to get the building up to plate high level, ready for the carpenters to commence work, who were booked to turn up the next day.

It was pouring with rain that day when I left home to go to the bungalow and so I prayed very hard on the journey to the site that the rain might stop so that we could finish the brickwork, ready for the carpenters to commence work on forming the roof.

As I drew nearer to the site my bricklayer and I could see the sky was still full of rain clouds but there was a small opening in the clouds with blue sky above and wonder of wonders that blue patch of sky was over the bungalow I was building.

It did not rain on us or the bungalow until after we had finished the necessary bricklaying work. It was raining all around but not on the bungalow and so again God gave me another miracle meeting a very real need.

Last but not least was a miracle we were given regarding finance. I had purchased a plot of land in Llanelli, Wales, that had originally been a yard for lorries, right opposite the Llanelli station railway line. I applied for and received planning permission to build five linked houses on the land and I asked for and readily received bank finance.

I started building the whole block of five properties bringing them all up at the same level of work. However, one day a member of staff from the bank came along and asked how many of the five properties I had sold. I replied that I had not sold any yet, I was waiting until there was a property of any significance for potential customers to see and appreciate.

It was not long after that that the bank advised that it was withdrawing its finance, as we had not yet sold any of the properties.

This was terrible news and an enormous blow, as I was building the five properties with the bank overdraft money, as agreed with the bank.

At the same time a housing association that I had approached wrote that despite what they had said before i.e. that they would like to buy the five properties, they had decided there were too many old properties that needed renovating in the area so they would not be proceeding to buy my five new properties.

My wife, with that devastating letter in her hand, said in faith, "I am believing they will change their minds."

We discussed the situation of the bank calling in the overdraft with our son and he agreed to buy one property with a mortgage, and we arranged to buy another ourselves, with a mortgage, so with the value of the two mortgages of the two properties, we were able to clear the bank overdraft, and not go into bankruptcy, for which we praised God.

I continued to work on the properties to bring them to completion and then out of the blue we received another letter from the housing association that they had decided after all to purchase the five properties in total.

God met the need, as the housing association did a complete turnaround and "changed their minds" just as my wife had said in faith many weeks before. We have a gracious God who is involved in every aspect of our daily lives.

+

Born in Perivale, Middlesex, I went to the same infant and junior schools as the young girl who later became my wife, Eileen. I was never a good scholar. I used to skip school or just deliberately be naughty so I would be sent home from school, allowing me to roam the hills bird watching, playing around the area or just being a general nuisance to the neighbours etc.

At just before sixteen years of age, the father of my girlfriend Eileen asked me what profession I really would like to follow, as I was in the boy's training pool at the Guinness brewery in Park Royal, Hangar Lane, Middlesex where only a few boy entrants were given apprenticeships so getting them out of the boys pool.

I told Eileen's father that I would really like to be a builder and he said that he would see if he could get me an apprenticeship, which is what transpired. Just three weeks before I would have been too old to apply, my documents came through and I was taken on as an apprentice bricklayer/stonemason.

So I left Guinness's brewery and began an apprenticeship to become a bricklayer/stonemason which I really enjoyed. Good weather or bad, each day seeing that I had constructed something myself was so rewarding.

Later, I started to do little jobs for friends and neighbours and so finally some years on I was working full time for myself, and later I became a registered British National House-builder.

I have built houses in Great Britain and in France, where we lived for just over four years and the house we live in in Spain.

In my late twenties I had a personal encounter with God, when I rolled my car, over and over into oncoming traffic on a road that had only recently had tarmac and stone chippings applied. My car ploughed through oncoming traffic but I thank God that I never hit or hurt anybody or their cars, and when my car came to a halt, upside down, on the other side of the road, with the roof crushed to the seats, I was able to get out of the front windscreen, which had disappeared and on the road.

When I got out of that car, which was completely destroyed, the roof being squashed onto the front bench seats, which I had hung onto as the car turned over and over, I danced around saying "I'm alive."

That night I knew God was real and He was with me. It was like an Emmaus Road experience. It took some more years before I was filled with the Holy Spirit and I allowed God to direct my paths, instead of "doing it all my way" as a self-made businessman.

For ten years, since living in Spain, I have been the Mojacar branch president of the Full Gospel Businessmen's Fellowship International Organisation in Almeria, Spain and I have seen people strengthened in their faith through listening to some awesome personal testimonies and others come to know Jesus as their personal saviour, which is so rewarding.

Miracles

There have been many times in our family lives where God has shown his love and provision in some very difficult circumstances, but He brings us through victoriously as we are never left without hope or help.

David Templeman. Spain

Miraculous escape

8

David's Story – My miraculous escape

 I had been married nine years when I started to be tempted to have an extra marital relationship. It started with a chat with a woman on horseback who rode past the building site I was working on. This then led me to saying to my wife I was going out on a Friday night 'with the boys,' but that was a lie.

It finally culminated with me telling my wife I did not love her and I wanted a divorce. She was so devastated as she did not know why I was trying to get her out of my life.

She cried day and night but I had hardened my heart to her. She found that she could not carry on working as a secretary, and so had to tell her bosses the actual situation, and that she was going down to Middlesex, what is now considered as Greater London, to stay with her parents. Her bosses, in turn, told her they would keep her job open for her.

In London she got herself a very good job as a secretary to directors of a large firm in North Acton, but told them that her husband had said to divorce him but she was not doing so. They accepted the situation and she began work with a very good wage, she later told me.

I had really hardened my heart to my wife. Seeing her cry so badly I was unaffected showing no remorse, and of course she took with her our nine year old son, who had to leave his school in Sprowston, Norwich, Norfolk, where the teachers advised my wife to try and get him into the best school possible, as he was university material, even at just nine years old.

I carried on with the 'other lady', staying round her flat, being asked to visit her parents etc., but after seven weeks of no contact with my wife, I felt that I must telephone her, saying to the 'other woman' something that was very foreign for me, "It is as if God is interfering in our relationship." So I phoned the home of Eileen's parents and asked to speak to Eileen.

I said I should like to come down and talk to her, thinking beforehand that I would see whether I would take her back, as if she was on trial, and during the conversation on the telephone she said, "You know nobody could love you more than I do." That remark went straight to my heart.

It was arranged that I would go down on the Saturday and Eileen, unknown to me, had lost a considerable amount of weight, came down from upstairs in a bright orange dress, I remember.

I suggested we went for a ride in the car and on stopping in the car park of a local pub, I asked her what she would like to drink and somehow, I spilt it down the front of her dress, which was quickly excused. I then said, "I have something to tell you," and before I could say what I was going to say, she said, "If you have been with somebody else, I could forgive you, as God has twice given me an identical dream of you in bed with another woman, and I have thought if I had to find another husband, I would not know what he had been up to previously."

The relief was absolutely enormous, as I knew my wife very well and was dreading her response, as she was a very trustworthy, honourable Christian girl.

With that enormous hurdle wiped out, she asked me to tell her everything, so that in the future nobody could say, "Did you know that?" or "When you thought he was somewhere or other that was not the case." So nobody could bring up something to hurt her In the future. This I did, but said "This was why I wanted you to leave, as I was going with the 'other woman' before you left for London," none of which she had ever imagined, trusting me totally.

I asked If I could accompany her to Church the next day, which was actually held in Perivale community centre by the organisation "Come Back to God Campaign". It was after the service that Eileen´s sister gave me the book "I Believe in Miracles" by Kathryn Khulmann and Eileen gave me a brand-new Bible in which she wrote the words of Peter to Jesus, "To whom can I go, you have the words of eternal life". I put the book and the Bible in the glove compartment and there they stayed.

On the Sunday afternoon, I went back to Norwich, ready for work on Monday, and said my goodbyes to Eileen, her sister and her mum and dad.

I went to work as usual and never visited 'the other woman' during the week but was asked to speak with the her, so I called to see her on the Friday evening, before leaving to drive down to Perivale to Eileen and the family, who I knew were waiting for me with a nice dinner ready.

I stayed too long, due to being asked not to leave yet, over and over again, so when I finally did get away, I tried to make up some lost time by overtaking a long line of traffic, and on one particular road, in the dark, with many headlights of cars on the other side of the road facing me, I encountered a bend I was not expecting.

I braked and the car lurched one way, I fought with the steering wheel and it lurched in the opposite direction, another manoeuvre and then I had lost control. It rolled over and over into the oncoming traffic, all happening in a matter of seconds.

The car was a Renault, with the engine at the back, not the front as normal, with front bench seating. It was just a few weeks old and only the week before, when I had visited Eileen, she had said, "Don´t forget to wear your seat belt", but I had not done so again that evening, which turned out to be a blessing, for as soon as the car rolled, I was able to lie down flat on the bench seating, gripping the seat edge as the car ploughed through the oncoming traffic, then there was silence, or so it felt to me.

Upside down on a grass verge on the other side of the road I tried kicking out the front windscreen to get out, but I found there was nothing there, and so I crawled out through it, over the broken glass and there in the headlights of the car was the book "I Believe In Miracles" and the Bible. I was so excited as reality hit me. I was alive. I was practically dancing around. I was totally unscathed.

Other cars stopped, the police arrived shortly and people were looking for any bodies or injured people, but there was just me rejoicing, unhurt.

One lady was taken into a nearby house and given a stiff drink, as she was so traumatised seeing the car headlights going over and over and imagining the worst scenario.

The police asked me to go to their police station and make out a report, but as nobody was hurt etc.

nothing came of that, and it transpired that the road had only recently had new tarmac and chippings applied.

Having finished with the police, I tried to telephone Eileen, but could not get through, and Eileen, upon seeing that I had not arrived at the expected time, tried to telephone some numbers to find me, as this was before the days of mobile phones, and she found her parent's telephone line was absolutely dead. Her sister said, "I feel there Is something very wrong happening," i.e. the devil was at work.

Not being able to speak with Eileen, I tried phoning a family member who lived near me in Norfolk but that person was out and so I telephoned 'the other woman' who immediately dropped everything and came to collect me in her car, thinking that she had regained me, but that was not the case.

The next morning the telephone line in Eileen's parent's house was once again working and on phoning around she found where I was and I told her how I had had an accident and had written off the car, but that I was totally unharmed.

Eileen said, "I am coming back, I shall give notice at my work and we can re-enter our son into his school," which was exactly what we did.

Regarding the schooling of our son, having been advised by his Norfolk school to seek the best possible school for him as he had A1 results in all subjects, my wife had sourced a private school for him, after talking with the headmaster of the school we both used to go to, who very honestly said to my wife, "If your son is as intelligent as you have been advised, I do not think we could do him justice."

My wife, it transpired, was due to post the cheque for the school fees up front for the private school the following day after I phoned her up, and so she did not need to post the cheque, and lose that money. A God piece of timing in retrospect.

Eileen acquired a pale blue Ford Popular and returned with our son, and I had to tell her that I had written out a cheque for the car insurance of the now totally crashed car, that the cheque book was thrown out of the glove compartment along with the book and the Bible, and in looking through the cheque book I realised I had not posted the cheque to the Insurance Company.

Two weeks had passed since the comprehensive cover insurance had run out and I was unaware that I had been driving a brand-new car on just third party cover insurance since that time. Worse than that the third-party Insurance cover would have expired at midnight that night and I crashed the car at circa 9 pm, just three hours inside that time limit or I would have had no insurance cover and would have been totally illegal.

I suggested to Eileen that I should do as somebody had suggested to me, that I just put the cheque into an envelope and then post it and pretend it had got slightly delayed or something similar in the post, but my wife said "No, go and see the manager and tell him the truth."

You see, I had written out cheques to pay for building materials and handed them directly to the builder's merchants etc. but I had not made it to the post office to post the insurance renewal premium cheque, which was in the middle of the cheques written out and personally delivered.

The Insurance office manager, where my wife had previously worked, did not even wish to see the cheque book and said, "Just fill in the claim form" which was so amazing as I had accepted in my mind that we would have lost the total value of the car, as it was out of the comprehensive insurance cover and we would make do with the little blue Ford Popular. but God again showed me undeserved favour.

Some days after the accident, when I took Eileen back to the scene of the accident, we could see that there were deep grooves in the road, caused by the roof of my car, and then I took her to the garage where the wreckage of the car had been taken to and upon seeing the state of it she said, "It´s like a giant had hit the middle of the roof with his arm ", as the roof was crushed onto the bench seating in a 'V' shape and was totally ripped from the sides of the car.

Over a period of six weeks, all parts were brought from France and they actually built a new car, in essence.

That experience changed my life. It was like an Emmaus Road experience. I knew God existed, that He had saved my life and also saved the lives of other people in the cars coming from the opposite direction.

It had all been a painful time for Eileen, as she did not know what was going on, but Christians had been praying for me. My wife, I later learned, had prayed "Lord give him a heart of flesh instead of a heart of stone," and one evening, during those seven weeks apart, in reading her Bible, one passage jumped out at her, saying "He will not test you beyond that which you are able to bear, but therewith will make the way of escape." In other words, God had the answer to the situation; do not worry.

It was September 1971 and I was 27 years old when I had that miraculous escape, and I thank God that He saved my life, but also that I came to know Him as Lord and Saviour. I don't just believe in miracles, I experienced one, for which I am forever grateful, 46 years on.

David Templeman

*

David and his wife, Eileen, live in Andalucia, Spain where they have just celebrated their fifty-fifth wedding anniversary.

Amazing Grace

9

Tracy's Story - Amazing Grace

I first met Jan about five years ago when we began working together in a local church.

I had prayed for a new prayer partner and she had asked God to bring her a friend, as her new role far from her family was lonely and tough.

We got on well, strangely, because we really were like chalk and cheese, Jan being the *go ahead* type and me being, *hold on let's just think about this a minute!*

We prayed together regularly each week, sometimes at home and other times prayer walking the local area; and we often saw God working His purposes out for the people we prayed for.

These were often little miracles in themselves as we worked in one of the most deprived areas of the country; the people we ministered to were the most vulnerable and very broken.

However it is not one of those people God chose to perform a miracle for, no, it was for me!

Whilst travelling home in the back seat of Jan's car one summer evening, following one of our many nights out supporting others in need, I suddenly felt extreme discomfort and couldn't get away from the pain that was radiating across the left-hand side of my ribcage and back area.

No matter how I positioned myself or shifted in my seat the pain didn't lessen.

I didn't like to make a fuss and tried to ignore it for a while, but it gradually got worse.

I finally mentioned it to the people I was travelling with and a short prayer was said, but nothing happened.

By the time I arrived home I was even thinking of taking some pain relief, something I only ever consider as a last resort.

I went to bed still in discomfort and decided I'd have to go to the GP if the pain hadn't subsided by the morning.

What I had at first thought might have been something irritating in my clothing, or possibly an allergy to my washing powder, continued throughout the night, the pain growing worse.

There was no escaping it, I was so uncomfortable and hardly slept a wink.

That made my mind up and an appointment was booked with my family doctor early the next day.

It seemed like forever waiting at home until the allotted time and nothing helped ease the discomfort, paracetamol, hot water bottles and cool showers were all tried, but to no avail.

Finally it was time for my appointment and I went in to be examined by a delightful new young lady doctor.

She listened to my symptoms and looked at the area where the pain had started, and was a little perplexed as there was only a small rash, not much to show for the discomfort I was in.

She decided to call her colleague, my usual GP, to get a second opinion.

He came in and again I described what had happened and how this unbearable pain had just begun suddenly the previous evening. He asked a few more questions and then made his diagnosis...Shingles!

Oh no I thought, that can be really nasty. I'd seen others with the virus and knew it could be infectious too.

A few children had been off with the chicken pox recently at the local primary school where I worked, I thought the viruses might be linked.

My GP prescribed a course of medicine that I was to take straightaway to try to limit the spread of the rash and help with the pain.

I went directly to the pharmacy and then back home to take the first dose. I got back in my pyjamas and dressing gown to try to get more comfortable and settled to watching the TV to try and take my mind off the constant irritation. (If you've ever had Shingles I sympathise greatly!)

A little while later there was a knock at the door, and Jan's cheerful face appeared in my lounge. She could see I looked unwell and was still in pain even though I'd taken the medicine prescribed.

With that Jan said, "Get up and let me lay hands on you and pray."

I had already had prayer and it hadn't seemed to have had any effect, but I wasn't going to argue. I got to my feet and Jan put her hand on the area where the pain had started.

She began to pray that God would heal the Shingles and take away the discomfort and pain.

Almost immediately the irritation was gone and I felt nothing in the area where the pain had been so excruciating.

It was amazing that something that had begun so suddenly the previous evening had disappeared with the same swiftness.

I was a little unsure at first and waited for the pain to return, thinking I was only imagining that it was gone. I even put it down to the first dose of medicine kicking in. However, if that was the case, surely it wouldn't have been so sudden and why just as Jan laid hands on me and prayed?

No, this was no coincidence, I was definitely pain free and able to move about without any discomfort and there were no repercussions of the symptoms later that day, or ever in fact. I never took any more of the medicine or pain relief.

To this day I believe I was healed that day by a miracle of God, through Jan equipped by the Holy Spirit, and I can't explain it any other way. The 8th of August 2015 was and is a day to remember. The verse I have marked in my Bible for this day is Matthew 8: vs. 17

"He took up our infirmities and carried our diseases."

Jesus was able to heal and as His people on the earth we are also given the power.

I don't understand why He chose to heal me, whilst others don't receive healing as we expect to see it. That might be one of the questions I'd like to ask Him one day.

But, I can testify that I was healed that day without a shadow of doubt, and I thank and praise Him for choosing me.

+

Tracy Taylor, age 52, has been a Christian for the past 18 years. She has two grown up children and works at a local primary school. She is joint founder of TLC GY, a Christian outreach project in the Great Yarmouth area, and worships at Kingsgate Community Church.

God's provision

10

Ray and Marilyn White's Story -Home of Peace Children's Home, Kenya

A UK Church first became involved with this ministry in 2004 when it was just a room with a few children sleeping on the floor. In 2010 the church felt that they could not continue to support this work financially due to the many demands on the church finance.

After much prayer Marilyn agreed to take on the responsibility for all the finances and for the training of the staff. This was before TLC

Children's Trust was established. Marilyn is now the Chair of TLC Children's Trust.

Home of Peace is an Interdenominational Christian Children's Home. Marilyn is part of the management team and runs the home with our Home Manager Mrs. Hellen Akinyi . Marilyn is a trained Counselling Supervisor, a Children's Counsellor and a Business Manager with experience in handling legal work.

Marilyn grew up in Zimbabwe spending about three months a year for five years on a mission station and then moved to South Africa. She lived in Africa for 35 years before moving to the UK and loves Africa and African people and really wants to serve these vulnerable children.

As a registered Children's Home the children are placed with us by the Department of Children's Services and their placement is kept under review by the court.

We could tell endless stories about our children. They come from some really sad backgrounds. Some have parents who died as a result of AIDS, Typhoid, Malaria or other diseases and as a result they were left homeless and to had fend for themselves because their home village was too poor to take on an extra hungry child.

Some were taken by their family from their tiny villages in the bush and dumped in the town of Siaya because the family could no longer look after them. We are talking about children as young as three or four years old. Once in Siaya they were simply left and had to beg or steal to survive.

These children now have a home. They have medical care. They have clothing. They go to school. They are loved and looked after.

We will not identify what happened to any particular child before they came to Home of Peace. They are children and entitled to their privacy.

We believe that many will grow up to become significant adult members of society. Community leaders, doctors, nurses, pastors, etc and it would be wrong for their past to be waiting online to be held in their faces later in life.

This charity was started by us, Marilyn & Ray White, after we became involved with the Home of Peace Children's Home in Kenya.

At that time we were running a ministry called Christian House Sitters and because of the real need in Kenya we took the decision to donate all income from Christian House Sitters to the Home of Peace. God has blessed and this has now become an official UK registered charity.

As with any registered charity we have a group of Trustees who oversee the work and carefully scrutinize the financial records every month but on a day to day basis the work is done by ourselves.

Our registered reason for existing is stated as: "The charity's objects are to relieve the needs of orphans and other underprivileged children and young people in Kenya in particular but not exclusively by the provision of funds for food, clothing, accommodation, education and medical care".

We channel all our funds to the Home of Peace Children's Home near Siaya in Kenya. We are in contact with Home of Peace every day and Marilyn is on the Management Team and Chair of their Board of Trustees so we are able to verify where every penny is spent.

Since we started supporting this home we have achieved the following. This is in addition to providing the children with food, accommodation, clothing, medical care and an education:

Built and equipped a nursery room for the young children; erected a security fence around the property to protect them from predators (human and animal); provided beds, bedding, mosquito nets etc. for all the children; provided all the children who are of school going age with school fees, exam fees, uniforms, text books, note books etc.; repainted and repaired the dormitories; established a first-aid system which has reduced the money spent sending children to the local medical clinic for minor injuries; built and equipped a permanent kitchen in 2014.

In 2015 we were informed that the home needed to be registered with the Kenyan government and to meet their requirements we did the following:

We established a farm and provided chickens to supplies some of the basic food needed for the Home; built two additional washrooms; installed a water pumping and storage system to provide a reliable water supply for the Home; built a large temporary dining room / study area and furnished it with tables and chairs so the children have a place to eat and to study; built two additional dormitories attached to which there are a first aid/ sick bay, an office / counselling room and accommodation for two house mothers; installed electricity in the Home.

Developments so far in 2016:

We appointed Hellen Akinyi as our Manager; we appointed Mrs Anne Okalo as our Social Worker and Assistant Manager; we are building a new boys dormitory; building a laundry; building a study room for the children; putting in additional toilets and wash rooms; converting our temporary dining room into a permanent structure; we have purchased two sewing machines and employed a qualified seamstress to make all our children's play clothes, church clothes, school uniforms and the staff uniforms.

Also to repair any damaged clothing. This will save us a lot of money in the long run.

All our staff are now registered for the Government health Care scheme and the Government Pension scheme.

All supplies are purchased locally. We do not waste money shipping out things that they can obtain from a local supplier. This saves money and benefits the local community. We do however insist on detailed, official receipts and for items such as beds, uniforms etc. photographs showing these.

2016 A year of many miracles.

Last January we had our first batch of students go on from Primary to Secondary school. All our staff and children are now covered under the National Health Insurance Plan; Our staff are now registered under the National State Pension Scheme;

Following a major storm we had to undertake a major building project.

Financially it was a really difficult year with major expenses, the fall in the value of the British Pound and rising costs. We thank God for all those who responded to our appeal and helped meet these needs.

As we start 2017 we are not expecting any major projects (unless God shows the He has other plans) but we still face the daily need for funds to provide all that is needed for wages, pension payments, medical insurance, food, clothing, admin costs at the home, etc.

We believe that God will provide but He provides through people.

Just before Christmas we had a shock but God did a miracle! We were expecting ten students to need funding for secondary / vocational training and we were under the impression that a Christian charity that sponsored the secondary children last year would do so again this year.

We had been in contact with them for some months and they knew the need and the numbers but when the cheque arrived on the 21st of December it was for just six children. They said their trustees felt that was all that they could sponsor.

The students were due to begin their schooling on the 8th of Jan and by that date we needed to purchase their uniforms, equipment and pay their fees.

Their equipment included a bike for each of them as there is no other way for them to reach the school. The total cost was going to be £350 per student.

We had no idea how we could tell four of these students that their dreams were dashed and that although they had worked really hard and done very well at primary school their education would have to end.

As we prayed we felt God did not want us to make this known to all our supporters just before Christmas as we know many already give sacrificially.

Marilyn felt God wanted us to contact a very small specific group of people so we asked Him who to contact.

He gave her four names. Two of them immediately replied saying that they would each cover one student.

Then on Christmas Day we got a wonderful email from one of the remaining two we had contacted apologising and saying that they had not checked their email for a few days and that they would sponsor the remaining two students.

What a wonderful answer to prayer!

Further information is available on the TLC Children's Trust website at tlc-childrenstrust.org

The information above is an extract taken from the TLC Children's Trust website with kind permission of Marilyn and Ray White.

*

We are a fun loving Christian couple who have been in Christian work for over 40 years.

Marilyn was born in England but moved to Zimbabwe as a baby.

At the age of 16 she moved to South Africa. Ray was born in South Africa and grew up on a farm.

We met in Johannesburg and got married in 1966.

Ray worked in business for many years before joining the staff of Youth for Christ in South Africa.

He later studied at the Rosebank Bible College and at the Baptist Theological College of SA before becoming a church Pastor.

In 1982 we moved from South Africa to England.

In addition to his theological training Ray trained in Psychology (BA Hon. MSc. PhD.) and since moving to the UK he has lectured in Psychology, counselled for the NHS and we opened a Christian Counselling Centre which for 18 years.

We also trained over 800 people to Accredited Counsellor Standard. many are serving God all over the UK.

We are now officially retired and focus our time and attention on this charity, Home of Peace Children's Home, Christian House Sitters and Ray also has an active ministry preaching at various churches and running seminars by invitation.

Twelve Months to Live

11

Margaret's Story – Twelve Months to Live

It was 2001 when my life was turned upside down. I had discovered a lump in my breast the size of a satsuma.

I was working as a Practice Manager at a local doctors' surgery so felt I knew the system, what was involved, who I needed to see, and what would probably need doing. Even with that knowledge, though, I waited eight weeks before seeing my doctor.

Then came the usual round of tests and endless wait for results. When they came back as 'inconclusive' it was then arranged for me to have a Core Biopsy and I spent another anxious few weeks waiting for the results.

The Consultant at the hospital told me that once again the test was inconclusive, that she was going away for three weeks on holiday, and when she returned she would carry out some more tests.

By this stage I was consumed with anxiety and I refused point blank to wait for the Consultant to have her holiday whilst I agonised over what was going on in my body. I told the Consultant so, and walked out of the consultation in anger.

I thought initially I would go for a private consultation – whatever it took – rather than wait for the Consultant to get a sun tan while my life was in the balance.

Fortunately, because of my work, I was able to speak to a GP colleague and told him bluntly that if I didn't get a biopsy urgently I felt as if I would chop the breast off myself. He realised how desperate I was and made a couple of calls and was able to arrange for me to be seen at the hospital on the following Monday when the biopsy was carried out.

There then followed an incredibly hard ten day wait for the results. I checked the post and the phone every day waiting for an appointment to get the biopsy results.

Eventually I went to the hospital to see what I could find out, and had an unbelievable discussion with the receptionist who eventually confessed that the reason I hadn't heard was because they didn't have any appointments available to offer me. I remember bursting into tears in the hospital, feeling absolutely distraught that I still didn't know.

It was two weeks later that I received an appointment letter for the oncology clinic, and when I arrived for the consultation I was told that the appointment had been cancelled. I couldn't believe that I was being treated this way and I refused to leave. I just sat and waited until eventually I was seen by another Consultant, and I knew by the look on his face that the news was not good.

I looked him in the eye. "I've got cancer, haven't I?" He told me Yes, and that it was the worst grading, and invasive. I remember feeling numb as he began to explain what was to happen. The next day an Oncology Nurse came to see me and told me how bad the cancer was. I would have to have a mastectomy followed by chemotherapy and radiotherapy.

I didn't tell the nurse at the time, but I knew I would refuse the chemotherapy and radiotherapy. I had watched the awful effects of that treatment on my sister-in-law just eighteen months previously, and she had died anyway. I vowed I would not put myself through that.

I had the mastectomy on 10th August 2001.

I went to see my GP colleague at the practice and he told me I had twelve months at the most to live.

I then fell in to a pit of despair. I had two wonderful sons and I realised I would never see them get married or cuddle grandchildren. I became angry at God, demanding to know 'Why me?'

All I kept thinking was – I am going to die. I cried every day, sometimes all day and felt wretched and sorry for myself.

Then one day I felt a tremendous peace come over me. God said to me " I am with you always and will uphold you in every situation. I will be your strength, and give you peace and joy. Believe in me and trust me. Have faith because I am here for you TODAY and everyday".

I thought that perhaps at my funeral there would be a miracle and someone would come to know God through my death. I was the only one in a large family who was a Christian.

I went to my Church and sat at the back during a service when the pastor invited me to go to the front of the Church for prayer. I wasn't sure whether to go. I had resigned myself to the fact that I was dying, but it was the Church that was determined to pray for my healing.

I did go forward, albeit perhaps reluctantly. I was surrounded by prayers and love, and one lady was crying as she prayed, reciting Psalm 30. I cannot explain exactly how I felt at that time but I knew something was happening, and when I returned home I read and re-read Psalm 30 until I understood. God extolled the Church to pray fervently for one another, and that was what my home Church was doing for me.

The time came for my Oncology appointment to discuss future treatment. This was when I would tell them that I planned to refuse chemotherapy and radiotherapy.

I had been told that my previous Consultant had left and a new one would be seeing me. I knew that the new Consultant did not have a good reputation for his bedside manner, and so it was with some trepidation that I sat before him.

He looked at me. "I can't explain it, but the cancer is gone. You don't need any treatment".

"So it's a miracle?" I asked.

He would not admit that. But I knew.

I have been a Christian for many years, and I know God's love. I know that he answers prayer and is there with me in whatever my circumstances (I don't know what holds the future, but I know the One who holds the future!)

*

I have now been cancer free for 16 years, However, I do have Lymphoedema in my right arm from the after effect of the surgery but I am still believing that God will heal me of this.

Both my sons are now happily married and I have three Grandchildren that I adore.

I took early retirement from my position as Practice Manager at the surgery five years ago, and have since trained to be a foster carer in the last two years.

The saddest thing is that instead of celebrating my Ruby wedding anniversary with my husband Stuart I was dealing with solicitors for my divorce.

My decree absolute is due within the next two months. This I have found to be the most heart-breaking thing I have ever had to endure after 41 years together. I married for better for worst, richer or poorer, Stuart didn't.

My Faith is stronger and my relationship with God is closer. I can do all things through Him who strengthens me. (Philippians 4 V 13)

ACKNOWLEDGEMENTS

It has been very humbling to read these accounts of events in people's lives, and I would like to thank each and every one of those who have contributed to this book. I know it has been difficult for some, who have had to relive painful memories, and others who have opened their hearts to share their stories.

You don't have to be a celebrity or have a high profile to experience a miracle from God. The people who have shared in this book are just regular people you would pass in the street and from all walks of life.

There are amazing, life-changing miracles of healing, some of which are recounted in this book. Others are miracles of God's intervention when all seems lost. But a miracle is a miracle, regardless of its 'size' or 'impact'. We can read or watch wondrous miracles on the internet but it's good to remember that miracles occur every day in many ways and in many lives. A reminder to us all that God cares for us. We are asked to pray believing.

In Mark 11: 20 – 26 (NIV) we read:

In the morning, as they went along, they saw the fig tree withered from the roots. [21] Peter remembered and said to Jesus, "Rabbi, look! The fig tree you cursed has withered!"

[22] "Have faith in God," Jesus answered. [23] "Truly[f] I tell you, if anyone says to this mountain, 'Go, throw yourself into the sea,' and does not doubt in their heart but believes that what they say will happen, it will be done for them. [24] Therefore I tell you, whatever you ask for in prayer, believe that you have received it, and it will be yours. [25] And when you stand praying, if you hold anything against anyone, forgive them, so that your Father in heaven may forgive you your sins."

So I would like to thank:

Mike Selch of Indiana; David and Eileen Templeman of Andalucia; Juliet Hawkins of Zurgena, Spain; Janice Tapp of Norfolk, England; Bishop Dr. Jerry Lee Garza Taylor of Andalucia; Margaret Holmes of Sheffield, England; Tracy Taylor of Norfolk, England; Ray and Marilyn White of Somerset, England.

If you would like to contact the author, Jane Finch, for any reason or if you have a miracle you would be willing to share, you can do so through her website www.finchlark.webs.com

If you have found this book encouraging, please leave a review on amazon so that others may read these amazing testimonies.

There is also a website for the book:

http://.believeinmiracles.webs.com

Miracles

Printed in Great Britain
by Amazon